HERALDIC SCULPTURE

An arrangement of one of the three original sets of painted plaster models of the Queen's Beasts by James Woodford

Heraldic Sculpture

Illustrated by the work of
James Woodford

with an Essay on Heraldry in English Sculpture
by Harold Priestley

THE BOYDELL PRESS

© 1972 James Woodford

Published by The Boydell Press
P.O. Box 24 Ipswich IP1 1JJ

ISBN 0 8511 5004 7

Printed in Great Britain by Benham and Company Limited, Colchester

Contents

Foreword

Eric Bedford CB, CVO, *Chief Architect, Ministry of Works, 1950–70*

Heraldry—the science of armorial bearings—plays a greater part in everyday life than most people realise. It comes through the post-box with our correspondence—the postage stamp, the letterheading—from the City or Borough Clerk; on the wrappers of goods denoting the retailer to be a Royal Warrant Holder; the arms decorating the coins of the realm; as a symbol adorning and denoting a particular use of a building.

The science is governed by rules and regulations administered by the College of Arms. It appears more often in the form of coats of arms, being a group of signs and symbols in a design to denote a genealogical history of those who can hold and display such distinction.

For the designers working in the many varied fields of artistic endeavour who translate the work of the College of Arms into visual design, whilst exercising the freedom to design heraldic components within prescribed limits or the overall shape of the arms within its surroundings, the very nature of the subject demands a discipline which only a few are willing to accept. It is of little value to the abstract artist.

This book is concerned with heraldry in the field of sculpture, and in particular one man. James Woodford, Royal Academician and sculptor, the son of a lace-designer of Nottingham, had all the attributes required to develop the art of heraldic sculpture: an inborn, painstaking care for detail, a great liking from earliest childhood for floral and animal form—features so frequently used in armorial bearings—and a classical training in the light, shade and colour of modelling. His period of training at the British School in Rome brought him into contact with painter and architect students alike and convinced him that man and his buildings demand the use of sculpture and that architect and sculptor must work together in the development of city and town.

It is at the time of ceremonial occasions when heraldry in all its forms plays such a prominent part in the arrangements. At the Coronation of Queen Elizabeth II in 1953, the then Minister of Works (now Lord Eccles) instructed that this was an occasion when the designer in the varied fields should have the maximum freedom to provide a fitting setting for such an historic occasion. Heraldry had been used on previous occasions, the Lion and Unicorn appearing as finials to the buttresses of the earlier temporary buildings containing the robing rooms and marshalling areas at Westminster Abbey. For this occasion James Woodford was commissioned by the Minister to produce a series of life-size beasts, now so well known as The Queen's Beasts. The Lion of England bearing the Royal Arms stood as sentinel at the entrance with the remaining nine standing in line, as it were on guard, outside the large window lighting the interior. Armorial bearings and floral emblems and other heraldic devices were used in profusion in the scheme of decorations along the ceremonial route from the Abbey to Buckingham Palace, and much of its success was due to those parts of the work entrusted to the sculptor, James Woodford. For me it was the start of an exciting and enjoyable relationship and has been the source of endless pleasure not only to myself but also to my colleagues in the Ministry of Public Building and Works, during an official career. Since then, James Woodford has been commissioned on a number of occasions for heraldic sculpture both at home and overseas, notably his large bronze animals flanking the entrance to HBM Chancery at Teheran which are of particular importance.

In a world of economy and financial restrictions, the use of heraldic sculpture to denote the official character of one type of building may be the only legitimate means at the architect's disposal to adorn his otherwise utilitarian structure. It is important with such stringency that those buildings which are to be adorned in this way shall bear work of the highest quality, carried out with the utmost skill, yet observing the strict laws which form the basis of the science.

This book of examples of the work of James Woodford as an heraldic sculptor records a rare talent in this field and is published in the hope that those who are to follow will be encouraged to study and further this combination of art and science, since heraldry must remain so long as man exists.

Heraldry and English Sculpture

Heraldry and English Sculpture

Harold Priestley

In the year 1540 the last of the English monasteries were dissolved and their lands and property were taken over by the Crown. Between 1547 and 1553, when, by order of the then Government, Protestantism swept England, an end was made of all chantries and religious gilds. 'At the same tyme,' says the Greyfriars Chronicle, 'was pulled downe thorow all the Kynges Domynyon in every Church alle Roddes (roods) with alle Images and every Precher preched in their sermons agayne all Images. . . . And at that tyme was moche prechyng agayne the Mass, and the Sacrament of the Awter (altar) pullyd downe in dyvers Places thorow the Realm.'

The chronicler's brief statement does little to put before the imagination the picture of the enormous destruction that was wrought by this temporary religious change—the wanton smashing up of statues, the pulling down of thousands of rood lofts with their images, the crucifixes with the flanking statues of Mary and John of which not a single one exists today complete, the shattering of the finely wrought altar-pieces, the loss of generations of musical tradition with the burning of service-books. The Reformation in England robbed the country of a vast cultural heritage, and modern art is the poorer for it.

Of the arts of the day sculpture probably suffered most, for its ancient patrons, the monasteries, were no more. Of the nobles and the wealthier men, few would go to the expense of setting up costly memorials for themselves and their families when nobody knew whether or not they would disappear in the next religious upheaval. For these reasons sculpture saw no great renaissance during the days of Elizabeth I such as occurred in literature, art and music.

Without patrons art cannot exist, and the patrons of the sculptor in the Middle Ages were mainly the moneyed families—the nobles, the gentry, the richer gildsmen and merchants who filled the churches with their memorials. The most important feature of all these was the shield displaying the arms of the deceased, together with all that went with it—the helm and the mantling that flowed from it, the crest, the collars, wreaths, badges and knots, the figures supporting the shield and the motto beneath it. All these were to be seen on the ornate tombs of medieval days, decorating the tomb-chests, appearing on pillars, arches and canopies. Every person of quality was familiar with their pictorial language which revealed at a glance details of birth, standing and family connections for generations past.

When a fighting man was covered from head to foot in mail, his device on shield, surcoat or banner was the only means by which his presence or his whereabouts could be made known to friend or foe. In this way a captain of arms came to have his own device, as peculiar to him as a person's signature is today, and which he bore in war and in the tournament. This device was even more permanent, for it served as the basis for those of other members of his family, each of whom bore it with his own variation or mark of difference.

In time this language, for such it was, was far too useful to be confined exclusively to the warrior class, and at an early date in its history it came to be applied to others. Since each device was for one family only, non-combatant members were entitled to use it whatever profession they took up. Heraldic shields came to be adopted by bishops for their sees and by corporate bodies such as towns, gilds and livery companies. Apart from family use, this is the main function of the coat of arms today and the heraldic sculptor is almost exclusively concerned with designs for courts and courtrooms, for embassies and consulates, for public corporations such as county and borough councils, for banks and large business concerns.

It is not too much to say that in the Middle Ages every sculptor, carver and metalworker had to be expert in heraldry. Its association with architecture made it a beautiful form of decoration as well as a historical record. The shields in the wall arcades of the nave aisles in the Abbey Church of Westminster are an early example. Sixteen of these, representing mostly the arms of benefactors to the building, including the supposed shield of Edward the Confessor, those of the Kings of England, Scotland and France, the Emperor of the Holy Roman Empire and many English magnates are carved in light relief and are represented, each suspended by straps from two miniature heads. Twenty-four more, executed much later, not carved, but painted, were disposed in the remaining bays. The gatehouse of Kirkham Priory (1289–96) is decorated with a number of shields including those of England, Clare (Pembroke), Warenne (Surrey), Ros and many others (Fig. 1). The benefactors to York Minster (fourteenth century) are commemorated by thirty-two sculptured shields, two in a bay, in the spandrels of the pier arches. St Albans Abbey Church has six, which are among the finest of their kind. Micklegate Bar, York, bears shields with the arms of Edward III.

In the fifteenth century came the erection of many fine churches and houses in the perpendicular style, and this gave ample scope for heraldic decoration on parapets, plinths and buttresses. The East Anglian churches of Wymondham, Blakeney, Swaffham, Long Melford, Cley, Aylsham and Lavenham have some fine examples, to name only a few. The rise of costly buildings in the sixteenth century was accompanied by an outburst of heraldic display as may be seen at King's College Chapel, Cambridge, the gateway to the Deanery, Peterborough (Fig. 2), and in the Henry VII Chapel at Westminster with its bronze doors ornamented with royal badges and Tudor roses, and its many ornate tombs (Fig. 3).

The decline set in in the later sixteenth century when the old nobility had largely passed away and new men began to rise in rank and wealth. These new men had to have coats of arms and it was a matter of prestige to possess a distinguished family tree. Such pedigrees were invented by the score and new achievements were granted. But whereas in previous centuries the heraldic shield had a practical value, to them its use was more decorative, and the heraldic artist was engaged to produce such things as ornamental chimney-pieces, tapestries, hatchments and other works executed in paint or embroidery rather than in sculptured stone. At the same time the simplicity and attractiveness of the heraldic device

1. The gatehouse of Kirkham Priory, Yorkshire

2. Kirkton Gateway, Peterborough Cathedral

began to disappear. Old families multiplied the quarterings on their shields until they were a confusion of design and colour while in new grants of arms such extravagances were allowed that many of them looked like picture-postcards rather than genuine heraldic achievements. All this points to a loss of knowledge of the first principles of heraldry. The expert sculptor of heraldic subjects virtually disappeared and his art suffered a decline from which, even at the present day, it has not completely recovered. In his famous work on *Heraldry for Craftsmen*, W. H. St John Hope complains that even in the memorial to Queen Victoria in front of Buckingham Palace there are glaring errors in the portrayal of the royal arms, and blames this on the general ignorance of the subject. Happily today this lamentable state of affairs is being altered through a revived interest in heraldry, the vigilance of the College of Heralds and the desire of public bodies to have coats of arms which shall be at the same time simple and of artistic value.

This tendency to increased ornamentation is shown in the case of the shield. Its original purpose was the protection of the body and the very earliest heraldic shield shows it in one of the best shapes for that purpose. The Bayeux Tapestry shows Norman knights carrying kite-shaped shields large enough to cover the whole body from shoulder to below the knee. In 1127, when Henry I of England knighted Geoffrey of Anjou, the husband of his daughter Matilda, the chronicler tells us that he hung about his son-in-law's neck a decorated shield. When Geoffrey died in 1151 a portrait of him in enamel was placed over his tomb. On it he stands under an ornamental arch in front of a richly diapered background, holding in his right

3. Gate to Henry VII Chapel, Westminster Abbey

15

4. Plaque over tomb of Geoffrey Plantagenet, Le Mans Cathedral

*5. Seal of John Mowbray, Earl Marshal and Duke of Norfolk.
1442*

hand his sword, erect, and on his left forearm a blue shield like that of the Norman knights in size and shape except that the top is flat with slightly rounded corners. On the blue background are six lions rampant, standing with one paw on the ground, three paws raised and tail erect (Fig. 4).

As long as the shield was used in war it remained simple in shape. The medieval knight carried a shorter shield, generally termed 'heater-shaped' because of its general resemblance to the shape of the bottom of a flat-iron. In some cases it had a rather wider curve making a sort of inverted flattish arch, its corners either sharp or slightly rounded. Many shields this shape may be seen in the spandrels between the wall arcades of the nave in Westminster Abbey.

The heater-shaped shield is the one usually associated with heraldry, but there were many other shapes. When knights fought in tournament they bore shields which were as wide at the bottom as at the top, with edges often ornately curved and in the left side a deep notch in which the lance tested when tilting. These are often represented in sculpture, sometimes ridged, sometimes with the edges curled over in leaf-shapes and occasionally with sharp pointed edges top and bottom. In shape alone the shield lends itself to many varieties of treatment, some of which are shown in this book (see Figs. 6 and 47).

From early days women bore arms, but since they did not go to war they bore them not on a shield but on a lozenge or diamond-shape. Though these came into general use in about the fifteenth century, they were unsuitable for carrying heraldic figures because of the sharply sloping sides. On one of the earliest of these, that of Frances Brandon, Duchess of Suffolk (died 1559), in Westminster Abbey, one of the crosses has had to be almost entirely cut out (Fig. 7). A more modern example of this is on the device of Princess Margaret (see Fig. 39) where the arms of Scotland have been covered by part of the label.

Apart from the traditional carving in stone or wood the modern sculptor has a variety of materials at his disposal and also the technical knowledge to deal with them. He may cast his work in iron, aluminium or bronze and if necessary cover it with stove enamel in a variety of

6. Shields from the doorway of the George Hotel, Glastonbury

colours to resist heat and weathering. The medieval sculptor had as wide a choice even though all he did was in local stone much of which was subject to weathering, but by the thirteenth century dark-coloured Purbeck marble was being carried to various parts of England, especially to London, where Henry III employed a large number of marblers and polishers working on church ornaments. One of their finest products is the effigy of King John, now in Worcester Cathedral, carved about ten to fifteen years after his death in 1216.

In 1290 Eleanor of Castile, wife of Edward I, died, and in her memory Edward undertook the erection of crosses at all the places where her body had rested on its last journey to London, as well as a life-size effigy of the Queen in bronze. An English goldsmith, William Torel, was commissioned to undertake the casting of this, which was done by the *cire perdue* process, a method by which the finer details of the figure were tooled in wax on a clay model and a mould then made by enclosing the finished work in clay and running off the wax under heat in an oven. The effigy, which took two years to complete, was cast in a single piece.

One of the most striking memorials of the time is that of William de Valence (d. 1296) in Westminster Abbey. His effigy is of wood covered with gilt bronze plates joined together, the joins hidden by strips of filigree. Part of the bed-plate, with a diaper of enamelled lozenges of England and Valence, still remains.

As the manufacture of statuary increased, so did the desire for good, cheap materials. Purbeck marble was durable, but by the beginning of the fourteenth century other materials supplanted it. Wood was cheap, but it had a short life. From about 1290 to 1330 wooden effigies were being manufactured in London, and there are still many examples in churches in Essex.

It was soon discovered that wood could be made to look like marble by giving it a covering of gesso, or fine plaster mixed with size. On this it was possible to stamp patterns while it was still soft, and then, when dry, to paint in the required colours. The process could be applied quite as easily to stone as to wood, thus making the use of marble or even the best quality stone unnecessary if money was not too plentiful. Then in the early fourteenth century came the increase in the use of alabaster.

Alabaster is a kind of gypsum or sulphate of lime. In its purest form it is white and trans-

18

lucent and these qualities have been widely imitated in our own day by makers of bowl fittings for electric lights. The earlier alabaster monuments are much whiter than the later ones, which often show brown marks and lines, since they have been dug from seams which have been extensively worked. As a substance for carving, the main advantage of alabaster was its softness, its relative cheapness and the ease with which it could be worked, coloured and gilded.

Modern man appreciates the beauty of clean, fine-grained stone, possibly because for so many generations his buildings and outdoor statuary has been overlaid by layer upon layer of soot. Medieval man, on the other hand, was passionately fond of vivid colour. His heraldic tinctures were in the main five in number—or (gold), argent (silver), gules (red), azure (blue) and vert (green), but these he used to good effect in infinite variations of design. The heraldic devices which first appeared on the battlefield were later to be seen in tournaments, where they hung in rows from branches of trees and on the spectators' stands. The drab life of the medieval peasant was relieved by his visits to the parish church with its brightly coloured cloths, its gorgeous altar-pieces, vestments, sacred vessels, and especially the tombs of the local aristocracy. Today the images or effigies lie grey and battered on their tomb-chests, with no hint of the lifelike and colourful realism they once possessed, and the paint has long since scaled off their shields of arms.

Yet even today here and there we may see fragments still remaining which betray the splendour they once displayed. The effigy of William Longespee, Earl of Salisbury, in the Cathedral there, was once brilliantly coloured, with gilded chain-mail, bearing on the surcoat the gold lions of his ancestor, Geoffrey Plantagenet, on a blue ground. The canopy over the tomb of Edmund Crouchback, second son of Henry III, at Westminster, displayed more than 150 painted shields. Much of the original enamel remains to this day on the tomb of William de Valence (d. 1296), also at Westminster. On his jupon are chased a number of

7. Arms from the tomb of Frances Brandon, Duchess of Suffolk, Westminster Abbey

8. *Effigy of King John, Worcester Cathedral*

small shields, and his own shield which hangs at his side bears the picturesque arms of his family, blue and silver bars with, around the border, a number of tiny martlets (Fig. 9). The gilt metal bedplate under the effigy is covered with diaper in a pattern of lozenges on which much of the material is still bright. The openings in the tracery of the canopy were filled with coloured glass which rested on a backing of foil which gave it brilliance. On the effigies of King John at Worcester (Fig. 8) and Queen Eleanor at Westminster the settings remain where once glittering imitation jewels had been inserted and probably covered with glass. Here too the tomb of Aymer de Valence, the son of William, still displays fragments of its original vivid decoration in stamped gesso, and in one of the cavities at the base there still remains a small fragment of painted foil covered with glass.

THE medieval knight or commander carried his family arms into battle on his shield and surcoat, and his followers wore his badge as their livery. When he crossed the sea the sails of his ship were bright with the heraldic colours of his device. When his remains were laid to rest in the tomb, his figure carved in stone or alabaster or worked in bronze, copper or latten lay on his tomb-chest in full armour, his feet resting on a lioncel or some other animal, his head on a cushion or on his crested helm, the shield bearing his personal arms at his side. Round his neck was the decorated collar denoting his rank or service. On his tomb-chest were carvings

9. Shield from effigy of William de Valence,
Earl of Suffolk, Westminster Abbey

in relief of angels, knights bearing arms or figures known as weepers, while, if he was rich, or famous enough, a canopy would be erected over it as lavish in decoration as the rest of his tomb. On it were all the main elements of his arms—the basic family design on the shield, varied in some small way to denote his position in the family; his helm and his crest. These, when combined with other elements—the mantling flowing from his helm, the supporters standing on each side of the shield, the scroll beneath it and the motto—form the combination known today as an *achievement of arms*.

The best-known achievement of all is the Royal Arms of Great Britain and Northern Ireland, its origins going back as far as the earliest days of heraldry. The shield, which is the original, and today the most important element in the achievement, has always borne the most famous of all heraldic beasts—the lion.

The lion, though not a native of western Europe, was known in England in medieval times. No doubt the knights who took the Cross were familiar with its appearance and well acquainted with its fame as an emblem of power which it had been from biblical times. Rampant, with paws raised, it inspired awe, and this is believed to have been its posture on the arms of Henry II. His son, Richard I, is believed to have borne two lions rampant, and later, in 1198, three golden lions *passant guardant*, i.e. walking, the front paw raised and the head turned to give a full view of the face. From that time onward the royal arms have always borne the three lions passant guardant on a red background.

In 1340 Edward III of England claimed the throne of France and placed on his arms the French fleur-de-lis quartered with the lions of England. The bulk of the English lands in France were lost in the fifteenth century but the fleur-de-lis remained on the royal arms until 1801. In 1603, when James I became king, these arms were again quartered with the lion rampant of Scotland in the second quarter and the harp of Ireland in the third (Fig. 10).

The present royal coat of arms, unchanged since 1837, is very simple. It is quartered, having in 1, the lions of England, in 2, the lion rampant of Scotland in a *tressure* or flowery border, in 3, the golden harp of Ireland with silver strings, and in 4, the lions of England. Between 1688 and 1837 it was varied many times to include such charges as the lions of William III and George I, the crown of Charlemagne and the silver horse courant of Hanover (Fig. 26).

Coats of arms have been quartered from early days. In the church at Hatfield Broad Oak in Essex is the stone effigy of Robert de Vere, third Earl of Oxford (d. 1221). He carries a shield quarterly gules and or (red and gold), and the mullet or silver star which is in the first quarter represents the star which is said to have guided his ancestor to the walls of Antioch when during the First Crusade his army was lost and in danger of being destroyed by the Turks. This effigy of a warrior clad from head to foot in chain-mail, drawing his sword out of its scabbard, must have been an awesome sight when it was bright and new, painted in vivid colours (Fig. 11).

Later, quartering became the most convenient way of placing two or more devices on one shield. The earliest example in England is on the tomb of Eleanor of Castile, queen of Edward I, in Westminster Abbey, which quarters the castle of Castile with the lion of Leon, the two kingdoms which were united by her father, Ferdinand III. This kind of quartering had, however, its drawbacks, for in time families intermarried to such an extent that shields came to be divided quarter upon quarter until they were no more than a confusion of small coloured shapes.

The lion, being one of the most common features of all heraldry, is worth special study. Medieval artists and sculptors gave it a heraldic form and, to symbolise the greatest possible energy, and ferocity, depicted it with large claws and a wide open mouth with tongue pro-

10. *The Royal Arms. 1603–88*

11. *Effigy of Robert de Vere, Earl of Oxford, Hatfield Broad Oak, Essex*

12. *Shields from the tomb of Eleanor of Castile. 1290*

truding, lengthened and curved its tufted tail and so arranged its limbs that even when walking it appeared fearsome. Welsh princes, who were a full century behind the English in developing their heraldry, were nevertheless quick to see the value of the lion as an emblem. Of all the memorials which remain in North Wales, three out of four depict lions rampant, most of these very badly done and looking more like pigs, dogs or cats. They are almost all too large for the field (or surface) of the shield and have had to have their heads bent unnaturally backwards, noses pressed against the upper edge, most unlike the modern heraldic lion.

In motion the lion was awe-inspiring; in repose he appears both powerful and dignified. He is an adaptable creature, capable of the peaceful calm of the Landseer sculptures in Trafalgar Square or of savage fury. He may be reduced to the simplest terms as he was at the time of the British Empire Exhibition at Wembley (1924) or by British Rail.

HERALDRY, which had its beginnings in Western Europe, has since been adopted almost the world over. Its use in the early Middle Ages as a means of identification was severely practical; in the later Middle Ages it became an important element in spectacle and ceremony. Following a long period of debasement a revival took place in the nineteenth century and this has continued to the present day. Old families and ancient institutions value their arms for their historical interest and the traditions they represent. These are added to year by year by achievements granted to newly created peers, to town corporations, county councils, industrial enterprises, public bodies and governments. To the artist, sculpture and architect they are valuable as a means of decoration; to the citizen or the member of a society they are pictorial symbols, each one a focus of some loyalty or other from school or college to nation and state. These are some of the reasons why it has found a prominent place in modern life.

Perhaps the most important reason of all is the possibility it offers for variety. The shield alone may be charged with an almost infinite number of geometrical shapes in different positions—the cross, saltire, chevron, bend, fess and pale to mention only a few, together with smaller ones such as the lozenge, billet, plate, escutcheon, canton, tressure and fret, or it may be divided vertically, horizontally, quarterly and in many other ways. These are among the earliest shapes and of themselves could have no meaning. The shield of de Waldegrave divided vertically into silver and red halves, and the three red chevrons on gold borne by de Clare could not at first have been any more than a means of identification. When other charges such as human figures, animals, plants, heavenly bodies, ships, buildings and other man-made objects were added, the message it conveyed was clearer. The lion, eagle, beaver, pilgrim's staff and scallop-shell carried their own meaning. Many shields bore charges which were a pun on the name of the bearer. Sir John Oldcastle's was a castle with three towers, Sir Thomas More three moorcocks, Sir Thomas Boleyn (or Bullen) three bulls' heads and William Shakespeare a spear.

The arms of a family were borne by every legitimate male member of that family but, unaltered, they did not distinguish one member from another, a thing which was very necessary when they were used in war or combat. This was at first done in one of many ways, as, for instance, the altering of the tincture or colour of one of the charges, the substitution of one small charge for another, the altering of the arrangement or number of the small charges on a shield or adding new ones either on the field or putting small on larger ones. Slight changes could be made in the shape or colours of crests, mantlings or supporters. Sometimes a chevron, a bend or a bordure was added which could be charged with various

24

small objects, and all these methods added great variety to family arms. The mark which eventually displaced all others is the label. This was borne by Edward I before the death of his father. In his case it was a narrow blue band with five short strips placed across the upper part of the shield. His younger brother, Edmund, Earl of Lancaster, used the label of France (blue with gold fleurs-de-lis) of four pieces. Later the colour of all labels was argent (or white), of three pieces only and wider than the original ones. In the early part of the sixteenth century the use of these 'marks of cadency', as they were called, was standardised, the eldest son only having the label, while others added different charges, for the second son a crescent, for the third son a mullet, for the fourth a martlet, for the fifth an annulet or ring, for the sixth the fleur-de-lis and so on. All children of the royal family, however, still bear the label as is seen on the arms of the Queen before her succession, and of Princess Margaret (Figs. 38 and 39). This label, always argent, is uncharged in the case of the sovereign's eldest son, and charged in differing ways for others. The uncharged label of the Prince of Wales is also on the necks of the two supporters and of the crowned lion crest. Princess Anne bears a label of three points, the centre one charged with a heart and the two end ones with the red cross of St George, while the label of Prince Andrew has one charge only, a blue anchor on the centre point.

The next in importance to the shield in a heraldic achievement is the helm with the mantling, the torse and crest that go with it. There may be a reason for its position above the shield. Imagine that a knight returns home after a battle or tournament. He is relieved of his shield and helm by a servant. The shield is reared against a table or bench either upright or at an angle and the helm is placed above it. The knight, who probably cannot write his own name, needs a seal for his letters and documents. He sees helm and shield placed thus and has them copied. The modern function of the helm may be explained from studying another coat of arms, that of the Devon County Council (Fig. 41).

The shield itself is symbolic, bearing the lion rampant and above it a ship resting on two narrow wavy bars to represent the sea, a reminder of Devon's long naval tradition. The helm, unlike that of the Royal Arms and the City of London, is placed in profile and the vizor is closed, like those of most corporate bodies, for the form of the helm is a sign of the rank of the holder. Peers have barred silver helms decorated with gold and placed in profile; baronets and knights have steel helms facing front with raised vizors, while the arms of a gentleman bears the same kind of helm as that of the corporate body.

Above the royal coat of arms is placed the royal crown, which consists of an ermine-lined circlet with jewels inset, on which are four crosses paty (i.e. with the limbs widening to their ends) and four fleurs-de-lis with two arches crossing each other over the crimson cap, and set with pearls, the whole surmounted by a cross paty of gold. Like the helm, the crown or coronet differs for the various ranks of nobility. The baron's coronet is a plain silver-gilt circlet with an ermine lining, set with six silver-gilt balls, four being visible, and a crimson cap. There are many other kinds of crown. The unicorn on the royal arms wears a crown-collar of fleur-de-lis and crosses paty, the lion rampant on the shield of the Devonshire arms wears the ancient crown—a plain circlet with four fleurs-de-lis, only one of these fully visible—while the crown over the helm bears three-turreted castles and unfurled sails with pennons, again a reference to Devon's association with the sea. The crown is, however, uncommon and restricted to persons and corporations entitled to bear it. The Corporation of Lloyd's, whose arms were granted in 1926, bears the device of the City of London and beneath it a fouled anchor, but it has neither helm nor crown (Fig. 40).

The helm, like the shield, was designed to protect a man from the blows of his adversary.

13. *Seal of Walter FitzWalter, 1415–31*

14. *Helm from seal of Richard I*

15. *Crested helm of Thomas of Lancaster*

The Norman helm, which looked rather like an inverted plantpot with two small slits for the eyes, gave way to the bascinet, with a pointed crown off which the sword-blow of an enemy might glance harmlessly. Sometimes the helm was ridged, and on this ridge was erected a fan-like steel plate. This is believed to have been the origin of the crest. The second seal of Richard I (*c.* 1198) shows his helm with a lion passant painted on the cap, and over it a fan-shaped metal crest (Fig. 14). A seal of Henry Percy in 1301 shows him riding a steed in full armour brandishing his sword. His crest is a wide-open fan round the base of which a scarf is tied and the ends flutter behind him like streamers. One of the finest early crests is that shown on the seal of Thomas of Lancaster. Both his helm and the head-armour of his horse are surmounted by a mythical monster known as a wyvern, its wings outspread and its long tail curled (Fig. 15).

From time immemorial the most common crest has been a feather or an arrangement of feathers; in some cases it is a pair of wings as in the crest of Walter, Lord FitzWalter (1415–31) (Fig. 13). Sir Sanchet d'Abrichecourt, a Knight of the Garter, had a bush or plume of feathers rising from the coronet in two distinct rows (Fig. 16). A bunch of many feathers either going to a point or spreading out is called a panache. A fine example is on the Garter stall-plate of Sir Simon de Felbrigge (*c.* 1421) in St George's Chapel, Windsor (Fig. 17).

To attract the female bird, nature has equipped the gamecock with scarlet comb and wattles. Man, following nature's example, turned the crest into an ornament, so that in joust and tournament the ladies might recognise and admire the pride and valour of their heroes. The crest under which a knight went to a tournament would have been an encumbrance in battle. Even more impossible would have been that placed on the helm of a hero at his funeral. On the Black Prince's tomb at Canterbury is a helm with a crest in stamped leather in the form of a lion with a tail of enormous length. On that of George Brooke, Lord Cobham, in Cobham Church, Kent, is the bearded face of a Turk, a twisted wreath on his head. Out of the helm of Sir Richard Beauchamp, Earl of Warwick (1439), rises the neck and head of a swan (Fig. 18). When crests became family ornaments, their size and detail grew out of all proportion to their original purpose. Old men, remembering the days of their youth and their exploits in the lists, were proud to hand them down to their sons.

The modern crest has kept its size and importance and is one of the most artistic features of the heraldic achievement. The royal arms repeats the lion motif, this time with a lion statant (standing) guardant, crowned with the royal heraldic crown. Devonshire has a crest depicting the head of a horse with a sprig in its mouth, and Lloyd's Corporation a ship riding the waves in full sail. This represents HMS *Lutine*, which was wrecked in 1799. Her bell still hangs at Lloyd's and is rung before important announcements are made. The City of London arms has a crest representing a dragon's wing of silver charged with a red cross, (Fig. 44). Sheffield has a lion rampant bearing between its paws a shield on which are eight crossed arrows. To come nearer to London, Enfield has the head of a stag, and Barking a representation of the old firebell or curfew tower with flames issuing from its base.

As the crest grew in size it had to be made separate from the helm and therefore some means had to be devised to fasten it. This was done either by a stout leather thong or by metal bolts, for there was in those days no such process as welding. In either case, the join had to be hidden in some way. Henry Percy tied a scarf round the join, but a more common way was to cover it with a piece of twisted material in a sort of circlet, and this is the form usually seen in modern heraldry. It is called a torse and there are usually six divisions showing how the material has been twisted and these are in the chief colours of the shield. A third way was to have the crest springing out of a circlet or crown which fitted on the helm. Many of these, with leaves and flowers rising from the circlets, may be seen on the stallplates of the Knights of the Garter in St George's Chapel, Windsor. They are known as ducal coronets though they have nothing to do with either dukes or with the silver-gilt circlet worn by a duke on formal occasions.

When a knight wore his helm, especially in hot climates, he was accustomed to cover it with some kind of a cloth or scarf which hung over his shoulders and protected his head and neck from the heat of the sun. This we believe to be the origin of what we call the mantling. In the case of the royal arms, it comes out from beneath the crown and sweeps upwards, dividing, each part turning on itself in graceful curves, sometimes ending in lobes like the leaves of the vine. The inner surface of the royal mantling is of ermine and the outer of gold. The earliest form of mantling that we have is on the stallplate of Ralph, Lord Bassett, whose shield is surmounted by his helm and a boar's head rising out of a ducal crown. From the rim of this crown a black mantling comes down and is gradually cut away in scallops until it finishes behind the neck in a simple tassel (Fig. 19). It was soon realised, however, that the mantling could be used to fill up any empty spaces, and on some achievements it completely surrounds the shield with graceful curves, adding richness and beauty. Its lining is usually silver, gold or some kind of fur, and the outer side one of the main colours of the shield.

Supporting the royal arms are the familiar figures of the lion and unicorn. This legendary beast (*unus*: one; *cornu*: horn) was believed to be very strong and fierce, and was readily used. Attached to the crown which acts as a collar on the heraldic unicorn is a chain which winds round the body and ends in a ring at its feet. This may be because it could be tamed only by a virgin, but when tame became one of the gentlest of beasts. It was part of the arms of the Beaufort family, and when James I of Scotland married Lady Jane Beaufort, grand-daughter of John of Gaunt, it is believed that it was introduced into Scotland, two unicorns being placed as supporters on the Scottish royal coat of arms. In 1480 the unicorn appeared on two of the gold coins of James III, which were known as 'unicorns' and 'half-unicorns'.

At the union of the two kingdoms in 1707 a crowned unicorn was placed on the royal arms as a supporter but the crown was removed after the Hanoverian succession in 1714. Two lions still support the arms of Scotland while the royal arms as used in Scotland has a unicorn, crowned on the left (or dexter) side, bearing the standard of St Andrew, and a crowned lion on the right (or sinister) side bearing that of St George.

The use of supporters was a very happy step in the development of heraldry. The earliest

are on seals. That of Richard, Duke of York, shows his shield suspended from the neck of a falcon while the shield itself is supported and enclosed by the horns of a stag.

The artist who made a seal had the task of filling a circular space with an attractive design, and the shield alone, or even the shield and helm, were not enough. The spaces on each side of the shield came in time to be filled in with figures, often taken from the badges used by members of the family. One of the first kings of England to whom supporters have been attributed was Richard II (1377–99), who is said to have placed an angel on each side of his shield and underneath it a white hart couchant (lying down). This beautiful little device was one of the ensigns of his mother Joan, the Fair Maid of Kent. The first king who is known to have used supporters in the positions in which we see them today was Henry VI (1422–61).

For the most part these early supporters are animal figures. In modern arms they stand holding the shield, but in many medieval shields they are obviously put there to fill in the space, for some stand above it, others appear to be clambering up to reach it. Where the shield almost fills the whole space of a seal the supporting animals are dwarfed, and then they seem rather to be hanging on to the corners than holding up the shield. Once, however, that the achievement of arms became an artistic creation rather than something to be worn or put on a seal, the supporters came to be a recognised part of it and now add greatly to its beauty and variety. They may be used on the arms of peers of the realm (but not life peers), by peeresses in their own right, by certain orders of knights such as the Garter and the Thistle, by county, city and borough councils and certain corporations, but they are not today granted to urban districts or to corporations below this rank. Some of them are exceedingly picturesque. Penzance Corporation bears a pirate and a fisherman holding a net, Sheffield bears Thor and Vulcan, the two gods associated with smiths; Devon a bull and a heraldic sea-lion (with a lion's head and a fish's tail) (Fig. 41), the Corporation of Lloyd's two sea-lions bearing tridents, the City of London two silver dragons charged on the underside of the wings with a red cross. Even more novel are the supporters of the livery companies of the City of London and those of the Commonwealth. Tasmania has two Tasmanian tigers, Jamaica a West Indian man and woman, the supporters of the Uganda arms are, on the left a male Uganda buck or kob and on the right a crested crane (Fig. 42).

Since the shield is being held up by supporters, the supporters themselves have to have something to stand on. Below the shield is a scroll bearing the motto, and in older arms the supporters are often made to stand on the two ends of this scroll. The arms of the BBC granted in 1927 show two eagles in this position. The lion and unicorn supporting the shield of the Prince of Wales stand on two circular golden frames which enclose the red dragon badge of Wales and the Prince's own badge of the three ostrich feathers. More recently it has become usual to place under their feet a strip of verdure known as a compartment, on which grows some flower or herb associated with the person or place. The Tanganyikan man and woman who supported the native shield on the arms of Tanganyika stood on a compartment representing the snow-capped Mount Kilimanjaro. The rose, thistle, shamrock and leek or daffodil are common features in the compartment of the royal arms of the United Kingdom.

Below the compartment is the scroll which contains the motto, which today must accompany every coat of arms in Great Britain whether or not it has helm, crest or supporters.

Stallplates from St George's Chapel, Windsor
16. (top left) *Sir Sanchet d'Abrichecourt; 17.* (top right) *Sir Simon de Felbrigge; 18.* (bottom left) *Richard Beauchamp, Earl of Warwick; 19.* (bottom right) *Ralph, Lord Bassett*

War-cries are older than heraldry, and some of the oldest and most famous mottoes, including the royal *Dieu et mon droit* (God and my right), came about in this way. Terse, meaningful sentences were sometimes engraved on the blades of swords, and it was common for noble families to have such phrases associated with them. The crests of Sir Simon Felbrigge and John, Lord Scrope, on their Garter stallplates in St George's Chapel at Windsor carry mottoes, and many others appear on seals.

In addition to their personal coats of arms most noblemen had badges which were worn on the livery of their retainers, and some of these badges carried short slogans usually expressing some sentiment. The Black Prince had a badge of ostrich feathers with the words *Ich dien* (I serve), ever since associated with the Prince of Wales. Henry IV, even before he was king, adorned his badge with the word *Sovereygne*. Words and phrases such as these may occur spontaneously, and then, too good to be lost, may find their place under some insignia or coat of arms. Thus it became the custom for the motto to be borne on the representation of a scroll running from side to side under the shield. As new achievements are granted, so new mottoes are continually invented. Many of them are in Latin, such as *Floreat Etona* (May Eton flourish), or the Canadian motto, *Ad mare usque ad mare* (From sea to sea), but they may be in any language.

From the fourteenth century onwards, heraldry was further enriched by the much wider use of badges, and many of these are pictured on modern coats of arms. The shield of

21. Badge of Henry Bolingbroke

20. Stallplate of John, Lord Scrope, St George's Chapel, Windsor

22. *Tomb of the Black Prince, Canterbury Cathedral*

Westminster, for instance, bears a golden portcullis on a blue field, and, above it, the arms of Edward the Confessor (who founded Westminster Abbey) between two Tudor roses. The portcullis was originally a badge of the Beaufort family and since Henry VII was the son of Margaret Beaufort (great-granddaughter of John of Gaunt) it became his. The story of the Tudor rose is well known. It is said that Edward I had a golden rose as a badge, that his Lancastrian descendants changed its colour to red and the Yorkists to white. When Henry Tudor married Elizabeth of York, the daughter of Edward IV, he adopted the red rose with white inner petals, symbolising the unity of the two houses, and this appears today in the royal arms with the Scottish thistle and the Irish shamrock growing from the same stem.

The badge, being simpler than the complete armorial shield, is older. The *planta genista* or broom which was worn by Geoffrey of Anjou never became part of any coat of arms but remained a badge of the English kings for more than two centuries. Edward II had as his badge the castle from the arms of his mother, Eleanor of Castile. Among the many badges of his son Edward III were the fleur-de-lis of France, the stock of a tree from Woodstock, which had been a royal residence from Saxon times, the griffin and the Plantagenet falcon.

The best-known badge of all is that of the three ostrich feathers probably brought to England by Philippa of Hainault, queen of Edward III, which appears on the tomb of her eldest son, Edward the Black Prince, at Canterbury. Though others of her descendants bore it, it later became exclusive to the Prince of Wales. Among the badges of his son Richard II were the sunburst, the white hart and the Plantagenet sprig of broom. His gilt-latten effigy at Westminster is pounced all over with these badges (Fig. 23).

The Wars of the Roses, when every important magnate had his own private army, are specially important for the proliferation of badges, for, whereas the coat of arms was the private property of the family and could be used by none but its members, the badge became part of the livery and was worn on the doublets of all their retainers. The bear and ragged staff of de Beauchamp, the boar of de Vere, the black bull of Clarence, the white lion of Mortimer, the bull of the Nevilles and other famous badges were seen on many an English battlefield. Henry VII, who put an end to Yorkist supremacy and to the long-drawn-out feud between the two houses, symbolised his victory by a number of badges—the white greyhound of Richmond, the red dragon of Cadwalader for the Welsh Tudors, the dun cow of Warwick, a crowned fleur-de-lis, flames of fire, a sunburst, a falcon standing on a fetterlock worn by the Dukes of York, the portcullis of Beaufort, a crowned Tudor rose, and, for himself, a crowned hawthorn bush with the letters HR, since at Bosworth Field he had won the crown, which is said to have been found under a hawthorn bush.

Among the most beautiful heraldic works of that time are the bronze doors of Henry VII's chapel, the framework of which is ornamented at the intersections with large Tudor roses and the interspaces made up of pierced work representing many of these badges, including the daisy of his mother Margaret (Fig. 3). Other remarkable examples illustrating this outburst of heraldic display are to be found in King's College Chapel, Cambridge. Here, above the compartment of the ante-chapel, is the royal arms, with Henry VIII's supporters, the red dragon and the white greyhound between two panels bearing on the left, the Tudor rose, crowned, and on the right the crowned portcullis. Lady Margaret, the king's mother, began the building of Christ's College, Cambridge, shortly after 1505. Her arms, fleurs-de-lis and lions passant quartered, and her badges are to be found on the gatehouse, and on the gatehouse of her later foundation, St John's College, the same arms are displayed with a coronet of roses and fleurs-de-lis over the shield (Fig. 24).

Many of the animals on these badges became the originals of the various groups of royal beasts. The medieval workers in stone, metal and alabaster were well able to construct figures in the round, for they had worked for centuries on effigies, even giving them the illusion of movement as in the kneeling figure of Lord Despenser at Tewkesbury, who faces the altar there in an attitude of prayer. The figures on the Percy tomb at Beverley (1342–5) are under-cut to such an extent that they almost seem to step out of their backgrounds. Animals were not strange to them, for they were expert in cutting these in relief and in the round at the heads and feet of effigies (Fig. 25).

Apart from these the earliest sculptured animals are to be found in connection with banners. It was natural that the captain of arms who had carried his banner through many actions should wish to have it set up on the gables of his house, or to use it as a weathervane. Carved animal figures were often used to hold these in place. As early as 1237 Henry III had 'a certain lion of stone' set up on the gable of his hall at Windsor Castle. At the ends of the monument of Lewis Lord Bourchier (d. 1413) in Westminster Abbey lions and eagles hold up banners which display his family arms. In 1506 a contract was made for setting up the king's beasts to hold up the vanes on the pinnacles of the nave clerestory of Windsor Castle, and five years later for putting similar figures over the Lady Chapel there. In 1513 Henry VIII made war on France and took an army to Calais. He campaigned in the greatest style. His tent was of crimson and gold damask and on the great poles that held it were set up eighteen royal beasts, eight greyhounds, four lions, three dragons, two harts and an antelope. In 1536–7

23. Pattern on effigy of Richard II, Westminster Abbey

24. Arms of Lady Margaret Tudor over gateway of St John's College, Cambridge

other royal beasts were constructed of wood and set up on Rochester Bridge, probably in honour of Jane Seymour, who had just married the king. These were the lion, unicorn, buck, greyhound, bull, boar, dragon, leopard, talbot (hound) and panther. The unicorn and panther were supporters on the Seymour arms.

In 1526 Hampton Court was surrendered to Henry VIII by Cardinal Wolsey and the king immediately set about making it a fitting residence. Among the improvements he made was the setting up of large numbers of royal beasts. The accounts include payments for 'a lyon and a dragon in stone, standing at the Gabull ends of the said (Great) hall', for beasts to stand on the coping stones of the gables, for four lions, four dragons and six greyhounds standing on the battlements, for '2 grewhondes, oon lybert (leopard) sytting upon basys barying vanys uppon typys at the haull endes' (the turrets at the corners). The gardens were equally well populated with lions, dragons, greyhounds, antelopes, panthers, leopards, and 'foure Innycornes servying to stand abowght the ponddes in the pond yerd'. Altogether, inside and outside the palace there must have been scores of these royal beasts either painted or carved. Other beasts were set up inside St George's Chapel, Windsor Castle and, by Queen Elizabeth I, at Greenwich Palace. Many of these decayed or were taken down and some have been replaced in modern times. When, at the time of the Coronation of Queen Elizabeth II, it was decided to place royal beasts outside Her Majesty's entrance to Westminster Abbey, a

34

choice had to be made out of the large number which at some time or other have been adopted by the various kings and queens of England. It was finally decided to choose those which would best illustrate the Queen's descent. Since the Black Prince, Richard II, Henry V, Henry VI and Richard III were out of the line of royal succession, many of the more famous beasts such as the white hart of Richard II, the antelope and swan of Henry V and the white boar of Richard III had to be left out of the choice. The number was finally reduced to ten.

The last component of the royal arms is the Garter which encircles or frames the shield. Edward III in the early years of his reign wished to create an order of chivalry made up of knights distinguished for their valour in the lists and on the field. There are various legends dealing with the choice of name for this Order, but nobody knows the real reason. The fact that the original companionship consisted of the king, the Black Prince and twenty-four knights divided into two bands of twelve leads us to believe that the first to be chosen were those who excelled in jousting alone, especially since many of the famous warriors of the day, such as Sir Walter Manny and the earls of Northampton, Hereford and Suffolk, were not among the list, but were only elected later as vacancies occurred. Since the number of

25. Supporter and shield from Percy shrine at Beverley Minster, Yorkshire

Garter knights has always been limited and has been headed by the king, membership is considered a very great honour, so much to that Sir Winston Churchill chose it in preference to any title that could be given him. Since the reign of Edward III the Garter has always encircled the royal arms. It consists of a strap or band of deep blue with the famous motto *Honi soit qui mal y pense* (Evil be to him who evil thinks) edged with gold and fastened by a golden buckle, the end of the strap ornamented with gold and hanging just over or between two sections of the scroll. Members also wear the collar of gold, consisting of twenty-six Garters each of which encircles a red rose, alternating with interlaced knots. From the collar hangs the badge known as the George, representing St George slaying the dragon.

26. The Royal Arms since 1837

In recent years public interest in heraldry has grown, and new arms continue to be granted. Local authorities and large corporations, seeking to display them in a suitable and lasting form on and about their buildings, turn to the sculptor. The growth of the heraldic achievement with all its variations and accessories provides the material; its expression in stone, alabaster or metal is the source of his inspiration, and on it he creates new forms and variations.

In this short account the information on heraldry has had to be limited as far as possible to explaining the features which are illustrated in the following pages. It is hoped that a perusal of the work of Mr James Woodford will serve as an initiation into the more detailed study of heraldry and of heraldic sculpture in particular.

The Work of
James Woodford

The Work of James Woodford

1. *Coats of Arms*

The use of sculpture in general on buildings has steadily declined over the past century, due mainly to simplification of architectural design and a reaction against the ornamental excesses of High Victorian buildings. Heraldic sculpture, on the other hand, retains its importance, since it appeals to this same economy of design. A badge or coat of arms, being a kind of visual shorthand, provides at once a discreet and restrained form of ornament and an aesthetically pleasing means of identifying the function of the building. The adaptability of heraldic sculpture means that it can find a place in even the most austere scheme without disturbing the architect's intentions; in the hands of the skilful and competent sculptor the achievement of several items of a coat of arms can bring to the work all the vigour and vitality associated with other sculptural forms free from the discipline of heraldry.

Following his work for the Coronation, James Woodford has carried out a number of important commissions. At home, the building of a number of new county courts has provided him with the opportunity to design the royal coat of arms for a variety of settings. The materials used—wood, stone, faience and aluminium—sometimes in full heraldic colour, vary according to the location of the building. Often they reflect the character of the area or town in which the sculpture is to be seen, as for example in the faience used in the case of Hanley in the Potteries.

Another important field is that of embassy and other diplomatic buildings abroad. The old restrictions on building style, laid down from London with little regard for local conditions, have given way to a much freer approach. On major buildings, very varied solutions to the design of the coat of arms have therefore been possible. At the other extreme, the many lesser offices used by the Crown at home require a standard insignia, sometimes for buildings in temporary use, and Mr Woodford has also produced the standard model for this.

Work for civic and private patrons offers a wider range of opportunities for original treatment and design, and the pieces illustrated here show the varied possibilities of heraldic sculpture as both formal ornament and instantly recognisable trade mark.

In addition to the many individually designed buildings both at home and overseas requiring the application of the insignia, there are numerous occasions where buildings not owned by the Crown are often temporarily occupied for official purposes. Again it may be that the location or the design of the building does not merit or demand the effort involved in an individual rendering of the arms. In such instances and in appropriate cases the earlier practice of applying a copy of a standard coat of arms has been retained after some modification and redesigning. The modelling of the arms has been brought into line with the simpler and more austere buildings of the present day, and the heavy casting in iron has given way to lighter aluminium for ease of handling and transport. The Arms, in full heraldic colour, are produced in three sizes, 6″ by 6″ miniature, 2′ by 2′ 9″ and 4′ by 3′, and have been used on civic buildings at home and for the Diplomatic Service abroad, employing the appropriate size for the purpose required.

28. Kingston upon Thames County Court

A horizontal design, but with crown divorced to form a central finial to the fascia surmounting the main entrance, of which the arms becomes an integral part, adding to the three-dimensional effect of the vestibule. The arms and fascia are in cast aluminium with stove enamelled finish for surface protection and weathering purposes. The size of the arms is 6′ long by 2′ 6″ high.

29. Portsmouth County Court

Carved in low relief into the brick facing material of the building, the design appropriately fills the horizontal area of walling between the two entrance doors to the vestibule and general waiting space inside the building. The coat of arms is sited at ground level, being 10′ in length and 7′ 6″ in height, carved to a relief of 4″ in depth.

30. HBM Chancery Offices, Athens

A rectangular design cast in aluminium, set against a background of polished Chios marble. The shape of the arms, with the light and shade provided by the high relief of modelling, completes the total design of the vertical panel of marble and the dividing horizontal lines of the aluminium trim to the building. The arms, placed above eye-level, floodlit at night, are 5′ square and the depth of relief is 4″.

31. Hanley County Court

The use of faience, where the basic material is clay modelled to the required shape and size, coloured and finally burnt to a vitrified face to give lasting qualities, was considered to be most suitable in view of the location of the building in the Potteries. At the same time it demonstrated the use of the medium in the field of heraldic sculpture. The size of the panel is 9′ 6″ in length by 7′ 6″ in height.

32. Bow County Court

Designed as a free motif above the main entrance door, the royal coat of arms carved in Portland stone set in brickwork becomes the central feature in the principal façade of the first of the new post-war county court buildings. The use of the royal coat of arms as a means of decoration is reserved for those buildings with an official purpose, and a service of sufficient importance such as the judiciary. In this instance the relief within the field of the arms was kept low in view of the contrasting surrounding material, the size being 10′ in height and 8′ in width.

45

33. Royal coat of arms, Willesden County Court. 1968

Coat of arms approximately 9′ by 5′ cast in aluminium, placed on a panel of similar material between the main entrance and exit doors. The composition gives greater emphasis to the vertical than the horizontal, to be in keeping with the architectural shape of the panel which forms the background. The panel is of a lower tone. The depth of relief is 3″, and the modelling of a fairly flat nature. One of the features of the design is the employment of the motto horizontally, providing a supporting base for the coat of arms. The garter becomes an oval instead of a circle.

34. HBM High Commission Offices, Ottawa, Canada

The incised carving of wall surfaces is of ancient origin, and has been used for various purposes, such as recording events or panel decoration from the earliest times. This example, showing its use in heraldry, can be seen in the arms decorating the entrance hall to a ground floor suite of conference and exhibition rooms in Ottawa, Canada, so positioned to be also visible from outside the building. The arms, 9′ square, are carved into the wall of polished Canadian granite, picked out in gold leaf, giving a sparkle by day and by floodlight at night. They were designed by James Woodford, and the work carried out *in situ* by local craftsmen.

35. Consular shield

The use of a specially designed shield or lozenge for attachment to buildings accommodating consular officials overseas, recognises the particular branch of the Diplomatic and Foreign Service of the government. The shield is usually located over the main entrance to the Consul General's Office or Consulate, in whatever foreign city the consul resides.

Until recently the insignia, a design of Victorian origin, was painted on a metal background and stove enamelled, but, again, with the change in character of the buildings now being occupied, and the nature of the materials used, a new design using aluminium, with its advantages of reproduction and lightness, has been produced. The lozenge shape of the design reflects the oval of the earlier example, with the facility of varying the name of either Consulate, Consul-General, or Vice-Consul, contained within the lower section of the encircling frame or band.

36. Central Criminal Court, Old Bailey, London. 1971

Coat of arms 5′ by 4′ 2″; depth of relief 6″. A rendering of the royal arms to be cast in polyester-resin and placed over the judge's chair in each of the twelve courts. The ribbon and the motto are omitted, and a feature is made of the Tudor rose, shamrock and thistle at the base of the composition. The mantling is treated boldly, circling the garter and shield, surmounted by the royal crown. The modelling round the edges is so devised as to appear to be in the round, and to add depth to the rendering. It is placed on a wall surface which slopes outwards towards the ceiling of the court, and is designed to give a normal view from the floor level.

37. Royal coat of arms, The Law Courts, Croydon. 1966

The plan of the building, comprising two large courts and two groups of three smaller courts, naturally fell into a symmetrical arrangement, and this indicated a central position on the main entrance elevation for such an important feature as the royal coat of arms. This elevation contains large plain wall surfaces, connected by a simple rhythm of windows, and this pointed to a fairly large scale for the panel. It is carved in Portland stone, and is 8′ by 7′, the depth of relief being 6″, and in contrast to the granite of the façade, gives emphasis to its importance as the central feature of the elevation. The background is sunk to a depth of 6″ and the front of the carving retains the main surface of the stone.

50

38. Cheltenham College. Coat of arms of HRH The Princess Elizabeth. 1951

This design was governed by the fact that the mullions and stone panels were all in one piece, and the number of mullions, by dividing the stone into five panels, decided the design and size of the coat of arms, and enabled the supporters to be in scale with the surrounding architecture. Though these are not actually supporting the shield, they give the impression of so doing, and the floral motifs incorporated in the centre panels give a good base for the supporters and lead on to the designs in the outer panels. These two outer motifs are raised in relief so that in composition they appear to connect to the tails of the supporters and thus form a unified design.

39. Lincoln's Inn redevelopment, London. 1968

Coats of arms of HRH Princess Margaret and Lord Upjohn, both past Treasurers of Lincoln's Inn. Size 2′ by 3′ 6″. Carved in Portland stone, designed to replace decoration destroyed during the war. Placed on either side of the internal wall of the rebuilt Tudor gateway, the carving is on the same plane as the surrounding brickwork, to give solidity to the scheme.

FIDENTIA

40. Lloyd's new building, Lime Street, London. 1954

Coat of arms carved in Portland stone. Size 8′ by 9′; depth of relief 8″. It is placed above the main entrance in Lime Street, a very narrow thoroughfare with tall buildings opposite, taking away a certain amount of light. The relief is therefore bold, in order that it might be correctly interpreted from street level. This coat of arms is repeated in a smaller size over the entrance to the main hall inside the building.

41. Devon County Hall, Exeter. 1962

This coat of arms, 6′ 6″ by 5′ 6″, is sited on the main wall of the council chamber, surmounting the chairman's throne. It is carved in oak, with depth of relief 4″, and pierced to show the silhouette against a white stone background, to emphasise the composition, and to contrast with the solid wall panelling. Oak was chosen for the carving to harmonise with the architectural scheme, which incorporates the panelling round the lower part of the walls, and thus supports the coat of arms. The siting of the arms at a fairly low level governed the depth of relief.

54

42. Uganda House, Admiralty Arch, London. 1958

This depicts a crested crane, part of the coat of arms of Uganda, and is carved in Portland stone; depth of relief 3″. The design is sited over the doorway, and is based on a keystone shape. The depth of relief is governed by the height from the ground, which is approximately ten feet. The surrounding reeds are in bas-relief, and arranged as a background composition to the bird, and to harmonise with the keystone shape.

43. *Coat of arms, The National Bank of Scotland, Edinburgh. 1942*

The panel over the fireplace in the board room is carved in Honduras mahogany, and the depth of relief is approximately 3″. The thistles have been designed to carry the line of the modelling down to the ribbon and motto and so encircle the supporters and shield, helm and crest within the composition. The top surfaces of all the motifs in the composition are on the same plane, thus maintaining the continuity of the panelling round the room.

44. City Police Station, Wood Street, London. 1963

This is the chief police station of the City of London, and the coat of arms of the City was naturally selected to occupy a space over the main entrance door. The building is in Portland stone, also the carved coat of arms, the size of which is 6′ by 6′. It is supported by two brackets, and the front surface of these, together with the coat of arms, stands proud of the main surface of the wall to emphasize the importance of the entrance. The depth of relief is 6″ and is in character with the strong rustication of the walls, and the bold architectural treatment of the building.

45. Keystone, Barclays Bank, Cardiff. 1954

The spread eagle was one of the many signs used in the City of London and was retained and incorporated with the three crowns in the grant of arms of Barclays Bank in 1937. The design grows out of the keystone over the main entrance and the eagle is used as a focal point to make a striking and bold composition. The eagle is carved from a stone of 4″ projection, and the modelling displays all the aggressiveness of a bird of prey. The keystone and the three crowns are on the front surface of the stone. The daffodil and leek are the emblems of Wales.

2. *Three-Dimensional Pieces*

Much of the work of the sculptor is in three-dimensional form or free standing, and therefore less closely related to an architectural background than a coat of arms applied to a building. This type of work, with the effect of space and distance between objects, can be used to bring emphasis to bear at a particular point in an overall design, as with an entrance either to a building or open space such as a civic park or garden, where heraldic sculpture is usually seen. The advantage of this method of treatment enables the sculptor to bring more colour of form into his work, and the viewer to see his work in the round.

James Woodford employed this technique on a number of commissions. The example of free-standing heraldic beasts holding shields, on applied piers on either side of the entrance, can be seen at Wandsworth County Court, providing the only relief to an otherwise plain flat façade. Examples of free-standing heraldic beasts on piers to mark the entrance to important open spaces are those to be seen at Bolsena and Minturno in Italy for the Imperial War Graves Commission. At Bolsena a vertical lion of England is depicted slaying the dragon. The heraldic beasts holding shields surmounting the entrance piers to the British Embassy in Teheran were modelled horizontally to suit the setting of a background of mature trees fronting on to a busy thoroughfare of a capital city.

46. Bolsena Cemetery, Italy. 1950

The lion on supporting coursed stone column
was designed to be a guide to the British
Cemetery at Bolsena in Italy, one of the many
war cemeteries built for the Imperial War
Graves Commission after the second world
war. It is 7′ in height and provides a finial to
the column. It shows the British lion triumph-
ant over the dragon, symbolising the power of
good over evil. The upright composition of the
carving is an extension of the character of the
column to keep a feeling of unity throughout.
Carved *in situ* in local stone, it is one of many
sculptures carried out for the British cemeteries
in Italy.

47/48. Wandsworth County Court, London. 1969

Lion and unicorn, approximately 6′ high, and cast in aluminium similar to other metal details on the front of the building, and stove enamelled to protect against weathering. As supporters of the royal arms, they are placed on two brick piers either side of the main entrance. The composition is an upright one to be in keeping with the perpendicular lines of the stone panelling and the windows above, and forms the main feature of the elevation. The animals stand free from the building so that the side view presents a good silhouette. The modelled surface is textured to contrast with the plain surface of the building.

49/50. HBM Embassy, Teheran

The use of animals surmounting piers to give importance at a particular point such as an entrance to a park or state is a long-standing practice in most countries. The use of the animal supporters of the lion and unicorn as free-standing beasts, supporting a shield bearing the royal arms at the entrance to the Embassy compound at Teheran, is such an example. The bronze figures, standing 6' high on a 6' by 3' base, designed in this instance

horizontally, look outwards from a background of dense tall trees, on to an important thoroughfare of the capital city, an apt setting for heraldic beasts. They are modelled in great detail to be seen at close quarters.

51. Mascot for a motor-car

Made in silver, approximately 6″ high. The design is based on the coat of arms of HRH the Duke of Edinburgh, incorporating waves to support the design, and to symbolise his service in the Royal Navy. The lion with two tails is shown with its forelegs outstretched to support the shield, which is the foremost motif of the design, also suggesting the forward movement of the car.

52. Minturno British Cemetery, Imperial War Graves Commission, Italy

Lion and unicorn 6′ high, carved *in situ* from local stone, Travertine, at the entrance to Minturno British Cemetery. They are placed on brick columns 20′ in height, in the main thoroughfare of Minturno.

3. *The Queen's Beasts*

The street decorations during the time of the Coronation of Queen Elizabeth II were notable for the use of heraldic devices in a variety of forms, and amongst the most outstanding was a set of ten animals or beasts designed and created by James Woodford to a brief supplied by the College of Heralds.

These sculptures were placed externally against the walls of a temporary entrance to Westminster Abbey, providing robing rooms and marshalling space for the royal procession before entering the Abbey.

The beasts, sited at low level facing the visitors, appeared as sentries protecting the building against unlawful entry, bearing the armorial shields illustrating the royal descent of Her Majesty. The orginal versions were cast in plaster and painted. Since the beasts were considered as an integral part of the architectural design, they appeared in a stone colour matching the building behind, with the shields alone in full heraldic colours. Echoing the vertical lines of the temporary hall and of the west towers of the abbey beyond, they expressed the sculptor's conviction that there can be no division in the arts of sculpture and architecture. The scale was dictated by their surroundings, while the modelling was very detailed, since they were to be seen at close quarters.

The group of sculptures formed a symmetrical composition, and this arrangement prompted the introduction of a change in stance, and a varying inclination of the head, also in the supporting paws of the beasts, and the outline shape of the shield, to bring individuality to each design. These features are still to be seen in the permanent copies in Portland stone now standing in front of the Palm House at Kew Gardens—an appropriate and up-to-date setting for a set of royal beasts of medieval origin, in a garden of royal foundation.

53. *The Lion of England, bearing upon its shield the present Royal Arms of the United Kingdom*

54. *The White Lion of Mortimer, holding a shield of the livery of the House of York*

55. *The Red Dragon of Wales, bearing a shield of the Arms closely associated with Wales, four counter-tinctured lions*

56. The White Horse of Hanover, holding a shield of the Royal Arms of the United King-dom as borne from 1714 to 1800

57. The Yale of Beaufort, holding a shield of the Beaufort colours with crowned portcullis

58. The Falcon of the Plantagenets holding a shield of the livery colours of the House of York

59. *The Unicorn of Scotland supporting a shield of the Royal Arms of former Scottish kings*

60. *The Griffin of Edward III bearing a shield of the royal livery colours upon which is the badge of the present House of Windsor*

61. The Black Bull of Clarence, holding a shield of the Royal Arms as they were borne by the Sovereigns of England from 1405 to 1603

62. *The White Greyhound of Richmond supporting a shield of the Tudor livery with a crowned Tudor rose upon it*

Index of Illustrations

ACKNOWLEDGMENTS

The publishers wish to thank the following for permission to reproduce illustrations:
Royal Commission on Historical Monuments (Figs. 1, 2, 3, 6, 7, 9, 11, 12, 22, 23, 24, 25)
The Trustees of the British Museum (Figs. 5, 13)
Radio Times Hulton Picture Library (Fig. 8)
Frederick Warne (Figs. 10, 14, 15, 21, 26. From *Boutell's Heraldry*)
Department of Environment (Figs. 27, 29, 31, 32, 33, 34, 47, 48, 49, 50, 53–62)
Photo Arts (Figs. 28, 30, 35, 36, 38, 39, 41, 45, 46)
D. Greenall (Fig. 40)
Sydney Newberry (Figs. 37, 51)
Harold King (Fig. 42)
A. G. Ingram Ltd. (Fig. 43)
D. John (Fig. 44)
Imperial War Graves Commission (Fig. 52)